Original title:
Sappy Stories

Copyright © 2025 Creative Arts Management OÜ
All rights reserved.

Author: George Mercer
ISBN HARDBACK: 978-1-80567-231-9
ISBN PAPERBACK: 978-1-80567-530-3

A Quilt of Dreams and Delights

In a town where the laughter flows,
A cat wore a hat with a big red bow.
He danced on the rooftops, quite out of sync,
Chasing a mouse who thought it could blink.

Old Mrs. Smith baked a giant pie,
Filled with odd fruit that made people cry.
She served it with ice cream that melted too fast,
And folks took a bite, saying, "What a blast!"

Young Timmy tripped over his own two feet,
Land on a trampoline—now that's quite the feat!
He flew through the air, just like a bird,
Landing in Aunt Edna's prize-winning herd.

In this patchwork town, where stories collide,
The strangest of happenings take quite a ride.
With giggles and grins, we'll share our delight,
For in every mishap, there's laughter in sight!

Serenades in the Quiet Moments

Whispers echo in the night,
A cat sings soft, a funny sight.
A squirrel dances on a wire,
While the neighbors play their choir.

Cups of tea and giggles flow,
As shadows play, the breezes blow.
Laughter sparks like fireflies,
In the glow of silly sighs.

Honeyed Words Beneath the Willow

Beneath the branches, secrets spill,
As candy hearts climb every hill.
A parrot mimics all our dreams,
While we plot our laughter schemes.

Kites catch wind with childish glee,
As frogs croak out their harmony.
We dance on air with silly tunes,
While fireflies light our afternoon.

The Diary of Kindred Spirits

In a journal marked with tea stains,
We record our high and low planes.
Each entry drips with mishap tales,
Where love's charm never fails.

We'll laugh at all our awkward phase,
As selfies freeze our cringy days.
With doodles bright, we sketch our dreams,
Planning trips with wild schemes.

Flickering Candles and Shared Glances

Candlelight dances on the wall,
As we trip over the phone call.
Each mishap sparks another laugh,
Like juggling plates, we share our path.

With cookies crumbling on the floor,
We hide our giggles by the door.
Silly moments mixed with grace,
In this warm and cozy space.

Maps of Where We Once Roamed

We drew our paths in crayon bright,
With arrows pointing left and right.
Each street was marked with silly names,
Like "Pudding Lane" and "Silly Games."

The places where we fought with sticks,
And climbed the trees to share our tricks.
Each corner held a hidden prize,
A place where laughter never dies.

Chasing Fireflies at Dusk

We ran like mad through fields so wide,
With nets in hand, our hearts our guide.
The glow of bugs, a dancing sight,
With squeals of joy, we chased the light.

But every jar we thought was full,
Would slip right through, how very null.
The fireflies laughed as we fell down,
In fits of giggles, we owned the town.

Starlight in a Glass Jar

We caught the cosmos in a jar,
Hoping to shine just like the stars.
But every night we'd see it fade,
Our brilliance dimmed, how quickly stayed.

We'd shake it up and give a sigh,
"Tomorrow night, we'll reach the sky!"
Each wish we made in secret tones,
Whispered beneath the moonlit cones.

The Sweet Taste of Reminiscence

We chewed on gum with flavors wild,
That stuck around, oh, how we smiled.
Like time machines in every bite,
Our childhood lives zoomed back to light.

We'd trade old stories filled with cheese,
Of epic fails and fallen knees.
With candy wrappers as our crowns,
We sat like kings, no fears or frowns.

Light Through the Mist

A cat in a hat was quite sly,
Chasing its shadow as it flew by.
In a puddle it saw its own grin,
Only to trip with a splat and spin.

Bright colors of laughter fill the air,
While frogs wear tuxedos without a care.
Each giggle a ripple on this sunny day,
As the sun dances on in its playful way.

Reveries of a Faded Photograph

Old friends in a frame, forever in cheer,
With faces so funny, we chuckle and leer.
That time in the park with our socks mismatched,
We'll frame that snapshot, our laughter attached.

The hairdos we sported, what were we thinkin'?
Like poodles in wigs, our fun was a-sinkin'.
Yet somehow, those memories make us all laugh,
Life's not just moments, it's a quirky giraffe.

A Melody of Longing

A kazoo serenade in the middle of night,
Is it music or madness? Oh, what a delight!
Each note is a giggle, a chuckle, a cheer,
While neighbors all wonder what's going on here.

We dance in the kitchen, with spatulas bold,
Twirling like whirlwinds, both daring and old.
The pancakes, they flip, like our hopes in the sky,
Sticking the landing? Well, we'll surely try!

Thoughtful Pauses in Silence

In the corner booth, a spoon sings a tune,
While cupcakes are plotting under the moon.
A sip of hot chocolate, a friend's knowing grin,
Leads to loud laughter, let the shenanigans begin!

With each thoughtful pause, the antics unfold,
As marshmallows dance and the stories are told.
In this perfect chaos, our hearts fly and sway,
Creating a symphony, brightening the day.

Memories That Linger Like Perfume

In the attic, dust and cheer,
Nostalgic whispers draw me near.
Old love letters, puppy paws,
Each page holds a laugh, a cause.

Lemonade spills on the floor,
While we danced, our dreams would soar.
With goofy grins and silly pranks,
We built our world with crazy flanks.

Faded photos, hats askew,
Every glance ignites the view.
Tickled hearts and teary eyes,
We reminisce, much to our surprise.

In the end, it's really clear,
We had the jolliest of years.
Through laughter's trail, we'll always roam,
These scents of joy, forever home.

The Last Leaf of Autumn

In a rush, the colors fade,
Golden whispers serenade.
One lone leaf clings to the tree,
Is it brave or just too free?

The wind ticks off each passing day,
With a cheeky grin, it starts to play.
"Fall like me, don't be a bore!"
But that leaf just wants to soar.

Squirrels chatter, plotting schemes,
While kids laugh, lost in dreams.
Will it fly with grace or flop?
Either way, it'll surely drop!

And when at last it hits the ground,
A crunch, a giggle, all around.
While seasons turn, we'll cheer with glee,
For each end brings more to see.

Paintbrushes of a Dreamer's Heart

With colors bright, we start to play,
A splash of joy in bright array.
Our canvases, a magical space,
With giggles stretching every trace.

Brushes dance with wild delight,
As unicorns take flight at night.
In every stroke, a funny tale,
As rainbows road, we set the sail.

A paper moon and dancing stars,
Our laughter echoes near and far.
We mix the hues of silly dreams,
With every stroke, the canvas beams.

Though the paint may stain our clothes,
We'll wear it proud; that's how it goes.
For every laugh, a color bright,
Our hearts paint stories, sheer delight.

Reflections in a Still Pond

By the pond where ripples gleam,
We share secrets, laugh, and dream.
Duck faces peep with quirky grins,
While frogs join in — let the fun begin!

With silly poses and splashing sound,
We set the stage for joy abound.
A frog jumps high, a splash of glee,
"I can jump more!" sings out with spree.

Mirror images, some wobbly sights,
Belly laughs on starry nights.
Our hearts reflect what waters hold,
In this laughter, life unfolds.

As the sun dips low in pride,
In every ripple, dreams abide.
With joy we leave this laughter's bond,
In the still pond, we forever respond.

Starlit Echoes of Affection

Under a sky of twinkling lights,
Two hearts giggle at awkward sights.
Whispers float like paper planes,
Wishing on stars to lose their pains.

Butterflies dance with silly grace,
Fumbling words, a blushing face.
Love notes scribbled on the lawn,
Turned into jokes by early dawn.

Cartwheels on Memory Lane

We rolled down hills, with shouts of glee,
Planting laughter beneath the trees.
Sticky hands from candy fights,
Chasing shadows into the nights.

Swinging high, we'd touch the clouds,
Wearing silly, mismatched shrouds.
Words of wisdom from a clown,
Life's a jest; we all fall down.

When Tides Turn Tender

At the beach, we built a fort,
Each wave crashed, a funny sport.
Sandcastles crumbled, pails flipped high,
Sea stars laughed as seagulls cry.

Salty kisses, splashes wide,
With jellyfish, we dared to slide.
A treasure hunt with candy maps,
Found only giggles and belly flaps.

Echoes of Laughter Under Moonlight

Under the moon, we danced and spun,
Telling tales of battles won.
Ghosts of laughter filled the air,
Jokes and jests more than we could bear.

A serenade of rhymes absurd,
Chasing shadows, we were heard.
With every giggle, dreams took flight,
In the warmth of the glowing night.

The Allure of First Glances

Two eyes met over spilled soda,
He laughed while she tried to hold on.
Uncertain hearts tangled in giggles,
It was chaos, but felt like a song.

A smile freed from a blushy fate,
He tripped, and down went his plate.
They shared a moment, clumsy yet bright,
Under the gaze of the food court light.

Love brewed in a frothy mistake,
As laughter echoed around the lake.
They played hopscotch on love's old tales,
Dodging pigeons, exchanging wails.

In slushy spills and cotton candy,
Their crumbs formed a love that's dandy.
For in the mess of first delight,
Laughter danced well into the night.

Petals on an Unwritten Letter

She found a note, or maybe two,
Written with a flower's hue.
But the words were lost, oh what a shame,
Only doodles and hearts remained lame.

He said it once with a ghost of flair,
Whispers of love hung in the air.
But each petal fell with a little sigh,
And their sweet words flew, oh my! Oh my!

In the garden where their sweet dreams grew,
Admiring each other like morning dew.
Yet shy hands fumbled like bees on a crush,
Turning red when the evening lights would rush.

A memory lingers like a hit or miss,
In jest, they chase a fluffed-up bliss.
For petals curled in the wind's soft play,
Can bloom into laughter, come what may.

Tidal Waves of Sentiment

A wave crashed with a playful splat,
He wore seaweed like a top hat.
They slipped and splashed in salty bliss,
In ocean's arms, how could one miss?

The gulls laughed as they took a dive,
Caught in the whirl, their love did thrive.
From wiggly toes to giddy spins,
A tide of giggles where fun begins.

As sand stuck like glue to their skin,
They built a fortress and jumped right in.
The sandcastle crumbled, oh what a sight,
Yet laughter echoed through the moonlit night.

With fishy tales and stories galore,
They danced in the waves, who could ask for more?
For in the splashes and playful swings,
Their hearts were light, just like the sea's flings.

The Canvas of Forgotten Dreams

He painted her name in the sky, oh dear,
With strokes of sunshine, bright and clear.
But clouds rolled in, a blunder bold,
And mixed hues of love with stories untold.

Her palette swirled with laughter and cheer,
Yet, splashes of paint made memories disappear.
Each canvas a giggle, a mishap defined,
A gallery filled with joy intertwined.

They tripped over brushes and fell in delight,
While colors merged in the soft moonlight.
With every misstep, their laughter grew,
Creating art from the wild and new.

In whimsical strokes and joyful screams,
They found their heart's wildest dreams.
For in the mess of a painter's glow,
They painted love, just letting it flow.

Daisies on a Windy Day

On a hill where the daisies sway,
Laughed a goat who thought he could play.
He chased after bees without a care,
Only to trip—oh, what a scare!

The sun shone bright, but oh, what luck,
A gust of wind made him cluck.
With petals flying, he did a dance,
While others giggled at his prance!

A squirrel chuckled from a near tree,
'That goat sure thinks he's fancy-free!'
He flopped and rolled in a sunny patch,
In a daisy chain that looked quite the match!

So watch the daisies sway and spin,
Among the laughter, let the fun begin.
Ready or not, the wind will blow,
Bring out the silliness, let it show!

The Weight of Unsaid Goodbyes

In a café, two cups sat alone,
While their owners chatted on the phone.
One said, 'I forgot my last line,'
The other sighed, 'Oh, that's just fine!'

They shared a laugh over crumbs and tea,
Remembering the tales of you and me.
But deep inside, their hearts did ache,
For words undone, a silly mistake.

A pigeon cooed, 'Don't fret my friends,
Life's too short for boring ends!'
With a flap, it swooped, grabbing a fry,
Leaving behind just a wistful sigh!

So cheers to laughs, and crumbs that fall,
To whispers of love, forget it all.
In the end, they'll both giggle and grin,
'Goodbye's not sad; it's where fun begins!'

Mists of Melancholy

In the mist where the shadows play,
A cat named Whiskers thought he could sway.
He leapt at the fog, a ghostly dance,
Yet tripped on his tail—oh, what a chance!

The crows above let out a caw,
Watching the spectacle with an awe.
Whiskers shook it off with a flick of fluff,
Pretending his tumble was really quite tough!

The moon peeked through, a giggling face,
As Whiskers tried finding his graceful pace.
But the more he stumbled, the more he won,
A furry comedian under the sun!

So in the mist, let the laughter ring,
For even the clumsiest cat can sing.
In errors, there's joy that we all can see,
In life's little blunders, we're all set free!

A Road Less Traveled Together

Two friends set off on a winding road,
With nibbles and giggles, their laughter flowed.
But a fork in the path gave them a scare,
One way was bright, the other quite bare.

'Let's go the wild way!' one friend did tease,
While dodging odd critters and swaying trees.
They stumbled upon a frog wearing shoes,
Who sang a tune that gave them the blues!

With every step further down the trail,
They met a snail who told quite the tale.
His jokes were slow, but the laughs did start,
And soon they found joy was the best part.

So here's to the roads that twist and bend,
Where the laughter flows and never ends.
In the wild and wacky, they found their glee,
On a road less traveled, just meant to be!

Echoes of a Crumbling Promise

A squirrel stole my sandwich, oh dear,
It danced in the park, full of cheer.
My friend laughed so hard, he fell on the grass,
While I chased the thief, oh what a farce!

We searched for a place to now have our feast,
With crumbs in our pockets, we feigned like a beast.
As pigeons eyed us with crumbs on our face,
We both knew this lunch was no normal disgrace!

The sun shone bright, we had fun with our plight,
But next time, I swore, I'd hold on so tight.
Yet squirrel's got the last laugh, darting with glee,
In the end, all that's left is this silly memory.

Sunsets Shared in Silence

Two friends with ice cream, flipped upside down,
They started to laugh as they both wore a frown.
With sticky hands waving in the warm evening glow,
They ended up painting each other like clowns.

The sun dipped low, and so did the cone,
A rainbow of colors melted alone.
They licked at their fingers, while narrating a tale,
Of epic adventures aboard a sea snail.

Behind them, the sunset was putting on shows,
While squirrels threw shade in their colorful clothes.
What a strange sight, two friends in a swirl,
Creating a mess, laughing into the world.

Tides of Melancholy

A fish that could sing, oh what a delight,
Swam by with a tune, oh what a night!
It crooned silly songs about jellyfish plots,
And how octopuses tied all their knots.

But soon the tide shifted, the laughter grew faint,
As seaweed grew tangled, impractical paint.
They spoke of lost treasures that turned out to be
A rusted old can, or a bottle of tee!

They gathered all shells, shared secrets from deep,
Like mermaids with capes who forgot how to sleep.
With each ebb and flow, they waved and they swayed,
In the waves of the silly, their worries allayed.

A Garden of Lost Whispers

In a garden of giggles, where daisies danced bright,
A gnome lost his hat in a hypothetical fight.
With frogs in the mix, that hat seemed to grow,
They swore it was magic, but seemed more like show.

Ladybugs chuckled, butterflies blushed,
As the gnome bumbled forward, he waddled and rushed.
They planned a parade for his non-existent crown,
But tripped over roots and fell down with a frown.

In this garden of whispers, the secrets unfurl,
Of friendships that bloom like soft petals whirl.
Though gnomes lost their hats, time turned out a friend,
And laughter and joy never seem to end.

Tea Stains and Forgotten Dreams

In a cup of tea, a secret brews,
A clumsy heart, a little bruise.
I spilled my thoughts on the kitchen floor,
While you just laughed and searched for more.

The sugar's missing, the milk has fled,
Our dreams are tangled; let's rest our heads.
We'll sip on chaos, a brew so rare,
Life's messy moments, a comic affair.

Every sip a giggle, every drop a joke,
Who knew our lives would thus provoke?
With each tea stain on the old tablecloth,
A tale unfolds, both goofy and froth.

In china cups, we find our fate,
Over mugs, we celebrate our state.
Though dreams grow cold and laughter wanes,
Our hearts still dance in tepid rains.

Threads of Yesterday's Light

In the attic lies a tattered thread,
A childhood blanket wrapped around my head.
With every pull, nostalgia shows,
It's hard to tell where laughter goes.

I chased my shadow, tripped on my shoes,
With friends like these, what can you lose?
The past spins tales of clumsy delight,
Like gummy bears on a summer night.

The sun flickers through the attic's small pane,
A silver lining to our playful pain.
With mismatched socks and a crooked grin,
We weave hilarity, allowing joy in.

In laughter's echo, the past feels bright,
Rewinding time in threads of light.
Though untidy tales may roam like cats,
We still find bliss in where we're at.

Flowers Beneath the Snow

Beneath the frost, a secret dares,
Impatient blooms with icy stares.
They shiver softly, thawing their dreams,
While squirrels giggle at springtime schemes.

Laughter tips the snowflakes' hats,
As daisies dance with fuzzy rats.
They poke through white, a gentle tease,
A sunny joke among the freeze.

Will he bring pollen, or just a sock?
The flowers wonder, while time does mock.
In winter's grip, a story grows,
Of love and laughter in frozen rows.

As seasons turn, the blooms come to play,
Spring giggles softly, it's a bright ballet.
From the snow's embrace, they take their stance,
Creating punchlines in the sun's wide dance.

The Sound of Your Voice in a Dream

In the land of snooze, where giggles lie,
Your voice floats by like clouds in the sky.
It whispers nonsense, a playful tune,
While my hair-do's dancing like a polka buffoon.

You're telling jokes only we can catch,
About dragonflies that are also a match.
In the dreamworld's glow, we float like cheese,
It's a laugh-a-thon, oh, such sweet ease.

Awake, I smile, still hearing your cheer,
In impressions of laughter, you reappear.
With morning light, our dreams take flight,
Like tickled feathers in pure delight.

In every giggle, a secret sings,
Of voices that dance on slumber's wings.
Your sound's a potion, humor's embrace,
As twilight whispers, we find our place.

Dancing Fireflies at Dusk

In the garden, they twirl and spin,
With tiny lights, they wear a grin.
Bugs in tutus, a sight to admire,
Who knew that they'd be such a live wire?

Sipping lemonade, I watch them play,
Turning my night into a ballet.
Giggles escape as they bump and flutter,
Their clumsy dance makes my heart stutter.

A firefly slips on a clover bright,
Sending his buddies into a fright.
They trip on petals, bounce off a leaf,
In this silly show, I find my relief.

As the night dances on, laughter rises,
A symphony of nature's surprises.
In this wild ruckus, my worries disperse,
And I'm reminded, it's fun to be terse.

Heartbeats in the Quiet Intervals

In moments soft, when silence hums,
A heartbeat stutters, then wildly drums.
Love letters folded, safe in a drawer,
Yet here I am, wanting more galore.

A wink exchanged, like magic dust,
In awkward silence, I start to rust.
A clumsy shuffle, a tripping shoe,
I laugh, you laugh, it's beautifully askew.

In the pauses where our breaths align,
A chorus of giggles, oh how divine!
We fumble and fuss, it's quite absurd,
But in this chaos, my heart is stirred.

So here we stand, in the stillness so sweet,
Two goofballs tangled, oh what a feat!
In tangled moments, we boldly play,
Finding the humor in every cliché.

Whispers of a Wistful Heart

Secrets shared under the midnight sky,
With every glance, we flutter and sigh.
A paper airplane thrown from the start,
Bounces around like my silly heart.

You tell a joke, and I snort with glee,
A moment so perfect, it feels so free.
Like rubber bands stretched, we giggle and sway,
In a world that spins on our whimsical way.

Our fingers fumble, in a race to clasp,
Butterflies giggling as we start to gasp.
A heart-shaped note, though ink spills in blobs,
Each smudge and each line is a playful sob.

With every whisper, we create a spree,
Painting our love with humor and glee.
For in this journey, so oddly sublime,
We're crafting sweet memories, one laugh at a time.

Golden Moments in Twilight

As the sun dips low, and shadows creep,
Laughter bursts forth, it's a playful leap.
Golden glimmers in the evening air,
In our world of giggles, nothing compares.

Through swaying trees, we skip and glide,
With silly stories that we can't hide.
We chase our worries like butterflies bold,
In this whimsical dance, my heart feels gold.

Fire pits crackle, as marshmallows fly,
And in our laughter, we forget to cry.
With silly faces and grins that gleam,
We mirror each other, a funny dream.

Twilight wraps around us, cozily tight,
In this crazy moment, everything feels right.
A world filled with whimsy, love, and flair,
In our golden twilight, we float on air.

Beneath the Surface of a Whisper

In the depths of a soft-spoken joke,
Laughter dances, words gently provoke.
A tickle in silence, a smirk that ignites,
As giggles escape through the cracks of the nights.

A blur of bright colors, a silly charade,
Mimicking quirks, the light-hearted parade.
With whispers that swirl like confetti in air,
Tickling eardrums, a sight hard to bear.

Beneath our murmurs, a giggling spree,
An orchestra playing just for you and me.
Wrapped in the warmth of a random inside,
Where humor discovers what we're trying to hide.

So let's spin the tales of our fumbling days,
As stars chime in chorus, in their zany ways.
For laughter glimmers in the silliest dreams,
Dancing together on whimsical beams.

Traces of a Once-Familiar Breath

A breath that lingers like forgotten cheese,
Reminds me of moments, those troublesome fees.
The scent of old socks and a popped balloon,
Whispers of laughter that float like a tune.

Echoes of blunders in every small gasp,
A ticklish memory, oh how we clasp!
With snickers and chortles as time slips away,
Those traces we carry, in clumsy ballet.

From hiccups to snorts, each noise has a flair,
Reminding us all life's a whimsical air.
The warmth of a glance, so oddly adorned,
In the strangest of moments, true joy is born.

So let us bask in this absurdity tight,
Share breaths of our follies until the night.
For in every chuckle, each laugh that we share,
We weave the hilarity, light as a prayer.

Mementos in the Quiet Hours

In shadows that linger, odd trinkets reside,
A sock without a mate, a mystery wide.
Treasures of chaos, a twinkling charade,
As memories whisper of the pranks we played.

The clock strikes a giggle in the hush of the dawn,
With antics of yesteryears, whimsically drawn.
Dusty old toys that still wear a grin,
Beckon us softly, let the laughter begin.

Each memento a giggle, a sparkling gem,
Brightening gloom with a whimsical hem.
Like plushy old friends, they embrace our delight,
In the quietest moments, stories take flight.

So here's to the treasures, the silly and stark,
That twinkle in memory, igniting the spark.
For in this collection of laughter we find,
Life's silliest moments, forever entwined.

The Weight of a Unwritten Letter

An envelope waits, with secrets inside,
A pen that just winks, but never complied.
The weight of the words hangs thick in the air,
Like fruitcake from grandma, too heavy to bear.

With each silent stanza, a giggle it hides,
Wishes and chuckles, like rollercoaster rides.
Unfolding the tales of our whimsical past,
In every pause, we're together at last.

The ink might be missing, the message unsure,
Yet laughter flows freely, a classic allure.
In blank sheets of promise, where humor can bloom,
We paint vivid visions that lighten the room.

So let the unwritten bring joy to the chase,
Our hearts filled with whimsy, our lives a big space.
For in every pause, be it silly or small,
The weight of our laughter outshines it all!

The Sweetness of Longing's Touch

In a café where time stands still,
A love note spills, my heart to fill.
I sip my tea, pretending it's fine,
While dreaming of you, oh how you shine.

A chocolate cake shared with a wink,
You take a bite, my thoughts just sink.
The frosting's sweet, but not as sweet,
As the way you laugh, oh what a treat!

We dance like fools in the middle of June,
While a stray cat watches, meowing a tune.
With every misstep, we burst out in glee,
Love's clumsy rhythm, just you and me.

So here's to the moments that make us grin,
To awkward embraces and where we've been.
In the garden of longing, we'll plant our seeds,
With blooms of laughter, fulfilling our needs.

Letters to the Moon

I wrote a letter, addressed to the night,
Telling the moon about our first flight.
With scribbles and doodles, the ink went astray,
He chuckled and winked, while I lost my way.

Under a tree, I whispered my dreams,
The squirrels gathered, plotting their schemes.
"Dear cosmic friend, I'm feeling so bold,
Send back a comet, or at least some gold!"

The moon just giggled, with beams that shone bright,
"Your letters are funny, oh what a delight!"
I sent him a cupcake, and he promised to bake,
A better dessert for our next little break.

So I'll keep on writing, each night just a tease,
To the moon, my buddy, who knows how to please.
And when I feel silly, I glance to the sky,
With letters of laughter, we'll never say goodbye.

Beneath the Maple's Shade

Under the maple, we'd sit hand in hand,
With bread crumbs scattered across the land.
The birds gave a concert, as squirrels pranced round,
While giggles erupted from where we were bound.

You'd tell me a secret, a joke of the day,
About a lost pickle who just couldn't stay.
The leaves whispered secrets of love, pure and sweet,
As we chuckled aloud, in our little retreat.

With lemonade smiles, we toasted the sun,
To silly pursuits and just having fun.
Our laughter turned echoes that danced in the air,
And even the sunlight seemed to stop and stare.

So let's make a promise beneath this grand tree,
To cherish the laughter, just you and me.
For in every giggle, the magic unfolds,
In the heart of the summer, our story is told.

The Colorful Threads of Memory

We stitched up a quilt of our wacky deeds,
With each little patch, a tale that still bleeds.
A rainbow of moments, both silly and bright,
Woven together, our fabric takes flight.

There's a square for the time we both tripped in the rain,
And ended up laughing, forgetting the pain.
With zig-zags of laughter, we tangle the past,
In a tapestry woven from moments that last.

The pumpkin spice episode, chaotic and fun,
When we crafted a pie and ate it all up.
With each slice we savored, a smile would appear,
Our friendship grew richer, with every cheer.

So here's to our patchwork, our colors combined,
With stories and giggles, forever enshrined.
In the quilt of our lives, may joy be our thread,
Stitched up with laughter, as our hearts are led.

Embracing the Ghosts of Yesterday

In a dusty room, I found a shoe,
It danced alone, as if it knew.
Old quirks and laughs, they linger still,
With memories wrapped around the quill.

A toaster burned the bread last night,
And claimed it cooked it just right.
The cat in a hat gave me a grin,
Who knew such style could cause a spin?

A love note stuck beneath the bed,
From a ghost who simply can't be dead.
His laugh echoes, a comical tease,
As I chase shadows with a sneeze.

Every old tale, a riot to tell,
While the past's perfume wraps me well.
With twists and turns, oh what a jest,
I celebrate the odd and the blessed.

Ink and Tea

A teacup spills ideas on the floor,
While the pen prepares for a lively war.
Ink splashes like a raucous laugh,
Every sip a friendly gaffe.

The teapot whistled, quite a chime,
As I spilled both tea and rhyme.
Words wiggled like a jitterbug,
In a dance with a cheerful mug.

Witty quotes float like steam,
Words colliding in a bubbling dream.
Scribbles mingling, a poetic spree,
With tea leaves weaving history.

Every draught, a swirl of fun,
In chaos where stories run.
In the end, with tea and ink,
Laughter bubbles before we think.

Radiance in the Rain

With every drop, the world goes slip,
Umbrellas turn to boats, let's skip!
Dancing puddles greet my feet,
As laughter ripples, oh so sweet.

The clouds above can't hold their glee,
Painting rainbows for all to see.
A soggy dog spins 'round a tree,
While I parade in poetry.

Raindrops join in a clever dance,
Inviting everyone to take a chance.
With each splash, a cheer erupts,
The gloomy weather? We interrupt!

So let the skies pour their best,
We'll stomp through puddles with zest.
In the downpour, we will remain,
Finding joy in the silly rain.

The Wayback Waltz

In vintage shoes, I take a twirl,
The past chuckles, give it a whirl.
A jitterbug in the living room,
As echoes of laughter start to bloom.

The radio crackles, a nostalgic tune,
And in the corner, a paper moon.
I trip on memories, fashion a bow,
Every step a story, a fun show.

In my grandma's pearls, I sway and glide,
With that wild spirit, I won't hide.
Her old stories snicker, a wink in their eyes,
Each twist through time brings a surprise.

So let's waltz back, where giggles reign,
In the quirky past, we'll break the chain.
Together we'll dance, no room for frowns,
In the wayback, we're the kings and crowns.

Echoes Through the Attic

In the attic where dust bunnies play,
Old love letters dance, in disarray.
A sock monkey grins with a cheeky wink,
While I trip on the memories—what did I think?

A mismatched pair of shoes from last fall,
They tell tales of trips, both big and small.
Under the beams, the laughter does swell,
As echoes of childish pranks weave their spell.

A forgotten toy with a heart made of fluff,
Still keeping secrets, though it's quite rough.
The ghosts of my past do a wobbly jig,
In this attic of oddities, each moment's big.

With each creak of wood and celestial sound,
I find joy in the chaos, sweetly unbound.
A treasure chest filled with giggles and glee,
In this cozy nook, it's just funny me!

Collage of Tender Moments

A photograph stuck on the fridge with a magnet,
Smiling like buffoons in a goofy bracket.
With mismatched outfits, we pose for the shot,
Captured forever in a moment so hot.

Cupcakes with frosting stuck in our hair,
Laughter erupts like we haven't a care.
Bubbles from soda, they twist and they twirl,
In the whirlwind of sweetness, my heart starts to whirl.

Knitting with yarn that was tangled and bright,
Two kittens dashed in, oh what a sight!
A collage of mischief and laughter galore,
Who knew tender moments could mean so much more?

Each thread of our lives, so silly and neat,
We stitch them together, a bond so sweet.
In this glorious mess, love takes the stage,
As we turn each page with a grin, not a rage.

The Secret Beneath Your Smile

Behind your grin, a mischief does lurk,
A twinkle in eyes, as you go to work.
Whispers of laughter, they tickle our ears,
Curious joy overflows with the years.

A cake made of cardboard, just for a joke,
With icing of paper, it surely provoked.
You served it with pride, wearing chef's hat, too,
As we laughed until stomachs ached, it's true!

A secret so sweet in a playful embrace,
Unraveled in giggles, no serious face.
Why take life too seriously, let's just have fun,
In this world of pranks, we're second to none.

Each chuckle a treasure, a light in the gloom,
As we dance round the room with a vacuum broom.
The secret beneath smiles, a riddle so bright,
Is laughter's the answer that fuels our delight!

Serendipity in a Cup of Tea

A spilled cup of tea on the floor makes a mess,
A splash landed on Uncle Fred's Sunday best.
With a wink and a grin, he plays the fool,
As sticky sweet moments become our own rule.

The kettle whistles, a musical sound,
We gather around, let the laughter abound.
With biscuits, we dunk, but oh, what a blunder,
A chocolate-chip plop, pure joy, what a wonder!

Each sip brings a tale, both funny and grand,
From spills to mishaps, it's all hand-in-hand.
Textures of friendship, brewed thick with delight,
In this playful dance, the day feels just right.

So raise up your cup to the magic of chance,
In every hot brew, there's room for a dance.
With serendipity warm as a pot's gentle glow,
Let's toast to the moments that help us to grow!

The Sound of Crickets and Heartbeats

In the dark, a cricket sings,
While my heart trips over strings.
A riddle wrapped in silly lines,
Love's a dance; here are the signs.

With every chirp, a giggle blooms,
Imagining us in grand costumes.
Two left feet but oh what joy,
Bumbling through, my clumsy boy.

The moon rolls over, grinning wide,
As we twirl on this bumpy ride.
In quiet nights, our laughter rolls,
Crickets keep watch over our souls.

So let the heartbeat and crickets play,
In this odd forest where lovers stray.
In tangled weeds, we'll find our way,
In hiccups and grins, we'll forever stay.

Traces of Laughter in the Silence

Underneath a starry hush,
Giggles escape in a joyful rush.
Between whispers, our chuckles hide,
In a cozy nook where hearts collide.

Every glance, a secret shared,
A playful tease, we've both prepared.
Silence thick, but oh so bright,
Like hidden sparks in the quiet night.

Oh, the pranks we gently pull,
A whoopee cushion, laughter's rule!
Caught in fits, we snicker loud,
In this silence, we're quite proud.

So breathe in deep this jesting breeze,
With every tickle, we find our peace.
In whispers soft, our laughter weaves,
A tapestry rich with joy, it leaves.

The Sweet Fragrance of Old Letters

Dusty pages filled with cheer,
Whispered secrets linger near.
Love notes penned in clumsy ways,
Each misspelling sparks a gaze.

Beneath the weight of faded ink,
A world of giggles makes me think.
Of how we brewed our grand design,
With lines that twist and intertwine.

The scent of paper, sweet and light,
Holds stories of our silly plight.
Every letter, a laugh to share,
Two hearts wrapped in a clumsy dare.

So let's be bold and write again,
With hued crayons and scribbles, then.
In this fragrant mess, we shall stay,
Creating words in a funny way.

Threads of Destiny Intertwined

In a tangle like my old shoelace,
Fate giggles with a cheeky face.
We weave our paths, a comical thread,
In the dance of life, we lose our head.

From silly falls to pie-in-face,
With every slip, a wild embrace.
Destiny chuckles, pulling tight,
Laugh out loud in sheer delight.

Round and round, the yarn unwinds,
Crafting chaos – oh how it binds!
Skipping stones, with jokes well-timed,
In this laughter, we are entwined.

So hand in hand, let's spin this tale,
With twists and turns that never fail.
In the fabric of joy we find our way,
In the threads of fate, we laugh and play.

When Footsteps Fade Away

In the park where laughter blooms,
A squirrel steals your sandwich, zooms.
We chase him down, in silly race,
As mustard stains our happy face.

Old man yells, "Get off my grass!"
Yet his own shoe's stuck—what a class!
We giggle hard, with bellyache,
Who knew lunch could cause such a quake?

The sun dips low, the shadows grow,
A frisbee flies—watch out below!
It lands right in the duck pond's dance,
And ducks quack loud, by mere chance.

With feet now wet, our joy won't fade,
In silly tales, our lives are made.
The laughter echoes, hearts are light,
In memories sweet, the world feels right.

The Once Upon a Time We Knew

There once was a prince who wore bright pink,
He danced like a goose, made us all think.
In a kingdom where vegans ruled with glee,
All bread was a carrot, can't you see?

A dragon insisted on gluten-free pies,
While knights brought cupcakes, oh what a surprise!
In fantastical feasts, we laughed all night,
As the jester juggled, it was quite a sight.

Cinderella's shoe was a croc, oh dear!
The ball turned into a wild buffet near.
We feasted and laughed till we could not breathe,
In this quirky land, we dare to believe.

So here's to the tales that make us all grin,
To dancing and dessert where the fun begins.
In stories that fuse both odd and sublime,
We cherish the joy, beyond space and time.

Yearning Under Starlit Skies

On a rooftop under sparkling lights,
We share our dreams and silly sights.
A cat in a hat trots by, what a view,
We wish on stars and play peek-a-boo.

A friend claims aliens stole his shoes,
While munching snacks, we laugh at the news.
The universe giggles, rolling its eyes,
As we dance with shadows, under the skies.

Each twinkling star tells stories untold,
Of legends and laughs that never grow old.
We sip on punch—an odd fruit blend,
Creating new tales as night's fun won't end.

And though the night fades, we'll never forget,
The laughter and dreams in our cosmic duet.
With hearts all aglow, we'll take one last sway,
Under starry confetti, we wish on today.

Threads of Yesterday's Tapestry

In a quaint old house with creaky stairs,
We sift through memories like tangled hairs.
With grandma's stories, we weave and spin,
Of a cat and a dog who played violin.

A postcard slips out, dated '79,
Shows us a party with zero good wine!
We chuckle loud, imagining it all,
As the cat in a hat guards the hall.

Each thread tells a tale of silliness true,
Of family feasts with a green, squid stew.
"Remember," we laugh, "when Uncle Joe cried?
Over a blender and fruit that had died?"

These moments together, like stitches, we bind,
In the fabric of life, love is entwined.
Forever we'll cherish these threads we adore,
In our heart's goofy tapestry, forevermore.

Chasing Shadows of Old Dreams

In a world where wishes float,
A cat wore shoes and danced a boat.
Jellybeans fell from the sky,
While giggles echoed, oh my, oh my!

Lemonade rivers drew a crowd,
With folks in swimsuits, laughing loud.
A parade of marshmallows marched,
Balloons and laughter, their spirits arched.

Chasing shadows, we all leapt,
In a field of daisies, while secrets slept.
Dreams twirled like ribbons in the breeze,
As we chased the absurd with utmost ease.

Every giggle pulled a string,
And oh, the joy that it could bring!
In a blink, our hearts outshine,
Chasing dreams, they feel just fine.

Stories Undone by Time

Once a tale of two wise owls,
Who hosted parties, wearing towels.
Dancing shadows played on walls,
As funny echoes bounced through halls.

With pancakes flipping high and far,
A squirrel sold nuts from a candy jar.
Time slipped by, the stories grew,
A circus of laughter, old and new.

Yet as the clock ticked its tune,
The owls forgot their silly boon.
A wise tale turned into a joke,
As daytime broke with wild smoke.

So here we are, with grins so wide,
Of tales that shift with the changing tide.
We laugh at the moments, sweetly obscene,
For stories undone are the best ever seen.

In the Heart of a Quiet Storm

A gentle breeze began to tease,
As rubber ducks sailed with ease.
In the heart of chaos, we find a space,
Where giggles surface, a silly race.

With a squirrel donning a cape,
He twirled and dove without a scrape.
Clouds in costumes drifted near,
Absurdity wrapped us all in cheer.

Umbrellas flipped in the jolly wind,
While cakes and rainbows began to blend.
Laughs echoed louder than the storm,
As we danced in the oddity's form.

In this whirlwind, we came alive,
Bonded by laughter, hearts to thrive.
The quiet storm showed a fun side,
In the madness, our joys collide.

The Gentle Kiss of Nostalgia

Socks and sandals danced on toes,
As children sneezed bright candy prose.
In the warmth of past days gone,
We spun like tops until the dawn.

A canary sung with a silly tone,
While alligators juggled stones.
Time tick-tocked in goofy ways,
Catching smiles with every phrase.

Through piñata parties, confetti flew,
With paper hats and jelly too.
In this kitchen of childish delight,
We feasted again, with hearts so light.

Nostalgia's kiss, a playful jest,
Wrapped us in blankets, snug and blessed.
As memories danced, we found our fun,
In the gentle warmth of the setting sun.

Between Pages of a Worn Book

In the corners where dust likes to dwell,
A tale of a penguin who danced very well.
He tripped on his flippers, fell on his face,
While a sea of fish giggled, they couldn't keep pace.

A cat with a monocle, sipping hot tea,
Critiqued all the fish on their lack of esprit.
With a twitch of his whiskers, he authored a guide,
On how to throw tea parties under the tide.

An octopus chef spun a yarn very grand,
Of spaghetti so tangled, it slipped from his hand.
Noodles went flying, a chaotic delight,
While the jellyfish juggled, their glow oh so bright.

So flip through the pages, let laughter arise,
Amidst all the nonsense, you'll find your surprise.
With giggles and chuckles, these stories unfold,
In the world of the silly, your heart turns to gold.

Whispers on the Breeze

A squirrel named Nutters wore glasses too thick,
He claimed he was plotting a tree-climbing trick.
But every time he leapt, he'd flop with a thud,
Leaving all of his friends in a fit of good-natured mud.

The flowers, they whispered their secrets so sweet,
Of bees who wore sunglasses when heading for sweet.
They'd buzz and they'd dance, pulling pranks in a swarm,
As the butterflies laughed, all in colorful form.

There once was a worm, called Larry the Bold,
Who dreamed of a life full of glitter and gold.
He tried to go swimming, got stuck in a shoe,
And his friends shouted, "Larry, the pond isn't for two!"

But laughter rang out on that warm sunny day,
As they gathered 'round, in their peculiar way.
For in every mishap, they found lots of cheer,
In the whispers of breezes, their joy was quite clear.

Lanterns on an Autumn Path

Beneath the bright lanterns that swayed in the trees,
A fox in a top hat recited with ease.
He told of a chicken who dreamt she could fly,
But just ended up pecking and bumping her thigh.

A hedgehog, quite charming, joined in with the jest,
Claiming he loved to wear sweaters – the best!
But each time he'd wiggle, his buttons would pop,
Sending laughter and threads scattering like drops.

A raccoon with glasses recounted a feast,
Of leftovers snatched from a picnic at least.
He danced with the moonlight, his belly a-roll,
While the owls booed and cheered, they were ready to toll.

So on this fine path, at the end of the night,
With lanterns a-glowing, all felt pure delight.
In the antics of critters, joy echoed along,
As they twirled and they shimmered, all happy and strong.

A Reverie of Long-Lost Laughter

In the attic of dreams where the dust bunnies play,
Lived a pair of old shoes who had danced night and day.
They twirled with amazement, on a floor made of socks,
As they chuckled at socks that resembled old clocks.

An umbrella, quite chatty, joined in on the fun,
Said, "I wouldn't get wet if you let me just run!"
But a gust of the wind gave him quite the surprise,
Sending him soaring, much to his demise.

A lamp with a dim bulb flickered a tune,
Of lovers who tripped in the light of the moon.
They giggled so hard, with a thump and a bump,
As they fell on the couch in a tumble and lump.

So treasure those moments, though foolish they seem,
For laughter and joy are the heart of the dream.
In a reverie visited by humor and light,
We find in the shadows, our spirits take flight.

Whispers of Sweetheart Nostalgia

In the park where we would play,
You threw a pie, what a day!
Laughter rang out, oh such a spree,
Sticky faces, just you and me.

Chasing dreams like kids at dusk,
Trading secrets, never just husk.
Your laugh echoed, a comical tune,
Beneath the light of a silvery moon.

A dance-off beneath the stars,
Your two left feet gave me the scars.
But oh, the joy, it pulled me near,
Yet you tripped and spilled your beer.

Memories like gum stuck to shoes,
Some sticky fights, but we never lose.
Holding hands, a wild embrace,
You pulled a face, what a silly grace!

The Melodies of Heartstrings

Singing off-key, we made a band,
You on the washboard, tapping your hand.
Off-pitch harmonies filled the air,
Neighbors chuckled, but we didn't care.

Your grandpa's hat, it was so divine,
Worn backward, oh how you'd shine!
A runaway cat stole the show,
As we tripped over in a love-lit glow.

Tell me how you love my socks,
The bright striped ones with silly clocks.
You'd tease me, say I looked so bold,
While we'd giggle, our story told.

Through crazy dances and silly songs,
In your silly world, where I belong.
We'll keep twirling, slip and slide,
With laughter in hearts, our joyful ride!

Unraveled Threads of Love

We knitted dreams with mismatched strings,
One looped in laughter, the other in flings.
Your scarf was bright, a patchwork craze,
Warmed my heart in the dusky haze.

Yet there you sat, a stitch awry,
With tangled yarns that made me cry.
But in the mess, love's hand we find,
Stiched together, hearts entwined.

Frogs in the pond, we'd yell, "Look there!"
As you leaped like one without a care.
All you caught was your own shoe,
And I burst into giggles, just like you!

Thrown together, like thunder and rain,
In every mess, we find no pain.
Hearts unravel but we hold tight,
This tangled mess feels just so right!

Rainbows in Yesterday's Eyes

Remember the day we painted the town?
Splashes of color all over the brown.
A rainbow born from splatter and glee,
With a paintbrush fight just between you and me.

Your socks turned blue, your hands all green,
A sight to see, oh, what a scene!
We danced in circles, a merry parade,
As laughter and colors started to fade.

You sang off-key, a charming din,
While I chased bubbles, letting them win.
Each pop a giggle, each giggle a shine,
Creating a tale that's ever so fine.

Silly moments woven with light,
In yesterday's eyes, everything's bright.
Through laughter and chaos, we bloom and sway,
With rainbows reminding us how to play!

When Time Paused for a Kiss

In the park where the daisies dance,
I hesitated, took a chance.
With a wink and a goofy grin,
Time stood still, let the fun begin.

Birds squawked out a silly tune,
As I leaned in beneath the moon.
A butterfly landed on my nose,
We both giggled, who knows where it goes?

The moment stretched like bubblegum,
As laughter echoed, feeling numb.
A clumsy shuffle, a funny slip,
We both fell, caught in love's strange grip.

But when I stood, the kiss was sweet,
Like cotton candy, a joyous treat.
In that instant, the world was fine,
Forever paused, you were mine.

The Taste of Summer Rains

Droplets danced on the pavement gleam,
Like little children, bursting with dreams.
Chasing puddles, laughter everywhere,
Splashing mud, freedom in the air.

A raindrop landed right on my head,
Made me laugh, like a clown instead.
With my gumboots, I stomped so grand,
Creating rivers where I could stand.

We twirled and spun through nature's show,
Each shimmer lit our faces aglow.
The wind joined in with a playful tease,
Carrying scents of summer breeze.

Oh, how the world felt light and free,
As we danced in joyful harmony.
The taste of rain, the smell of cheer,
Funny how love grows year after year.

Windswept Wishes in the Twilight

Under stars where secrets prance,
I made a wish with a morose glance.
The wind, it giggled, tangled my hair,
A swirl of laughter, caught unaware.

Clouds nudged each other, sly and coy,
As I whispered wishes, oh what joy!
A tumbleweed rolled just for the show,
Windswept dreams, blowing to and fro.

Each wish lodged like a silly song,
Crashing against the night, it felt so wrong.
Fireflies flickered in a silly tease,
Drawing shapes that danced in the breeze.

Then a gust hit, I lost my hat,
Grabbed it quick, oh how I sat!
In twilight's charm, with laughter pure,
Windswept wishes always endure.

Lanterns of Longing

With lanterns bright in the summer night,
We chased our shadows, oh what a sight.
I stumbled over then fell, quite a show,
You laughed so loud, it echoed below.

Old tales spun under stars above,
With every moment, we fell in love.
Your eyes twinkled like the lanterns' glow,
And suddenly, my heart went whoa!

We shared our secrets, close and tight,
Like lanterns hanging, they felt just right.
A ghost story slipped, I squeaked with fright,
You threw back your head with delight.

In sweet silliness, our hearts took flight,
Guided by lanterns in the peaceful night.
Together we laughed, like kids at play,
In lanterns' glow, love found its way.

A Dance Beneath the Stars

In a field where the moonlight plays,
Two clumsy souls lost in a daze.
They trip on their feet, a comedic sight,
Yet their giggles echo into the night.

A lopsided tango, they stumble and sway,
While fireflies tease in a playful display.
They spin and they twirl, quite out of control,
With each little fumble, they're stealing the show.

Stars wink down at their whimsical spree,
As laughter rings out—a contagious decree.
The universe grins at their joy in the dark,
Creating their own little spark in the park.

So dance on, dear friends, with a heart so true,
The silliest waltz is the best kind for two.
As the night softly fades, they'll cherish this night,
In the dance beneath stars that shined oh so bright.

When Raindrops Speak of Love

Upon the rooftops, raindrops parade,
Each one a lover, in splashes they wade.
With puddles of laughter, they slip and slide,
This ballet of nature, their joy they won't hide.

Umbrellas are weapons, a comical fight,
As they dodge and they weave, what a silly sight!
A splash here, a splash there, splatters abound,
In this rainy romance, pure glee can be found.

They chase after rainbows, with smiles so wide,
And count all the droplets as sweet love they bide.
With each little echo of thunder above,
They giggle together, oh, what a sweet love!

So let it rain down, let the fun never cease,
In these moments of joy, they find their own peace.
For love is like raindrops, a glorious game,
With each little plop, they'll never be the same.

Memories Wrapped in Soft Embrace

In a cozy corner with pillows piled high,
Two friends share tales and laughter that fly.
With every soft snicker, a new story born,
Of mishaps and giggles, they laugh until dawn.

Their blankets are shields from the world outside,
In this fortress of chuckles, they lovingly hide.
They snort like wild geese at jokes gone awry,
As memories wrap 'round like a warm apple pie.

Each tale is a treasure, a whimsical song,
When shared with a friend, nothing can go wrong.
Together they roam through their laughter-filled past,
Creating a bond that will forever last.

So here's to the moments wrapped up in delight,
To friends and to laughter that sparkle so bright.
They'll cherish these tales, as the years fade away,
In this soft embrace, forever they'll stay.

The Echo of Your Laughter

There's a bell in the distance, it rings with such glee,
It's the echo of laughter, and it's calling for me.
It bounces like bubbles, so light in the air,
With chuckles and snickers, in moments we share.

A joke turns to riddles, a good pun set free,
With you by my side, I'm just filled with glee.
We chase down the giggles, they scatter and play,
As your laughter dances like sunlight through gray.

In a crowd, we are partners, in our own little show,
Your humor's the secret that makes my heart glow.
With jests and with jibes, what a riot we make,
In the echo of laughter, it's memories we bake.

So let all the giggles and fun times resound,
For in every laugh, our joys can be found.
Each snicker, each chuckle, a sweet serenade,
In the echo of your laughter, my heart's serenade.

Illuminated by Your Smile

In a café, you spilled your drink,
My laughter made me think,
Your nervous grin, those eyes so bright,
Turning clumsiness to pure delight.

A slip of soup, a fall from grace,
You tripped and landed, what a face!
We laughed so hard, the waiter frowned,
Love bloomed where laughter drowned.

The flicker of a candle's glow,
Illuminates the silly show,
With chatter loud and cups in hand,
Together, we make quite the band.

Days pass by, and still I see,
Your smile is magic, just like me,
In every blunder, in every fall,
You shine bright—I love it all.

Remembering When Time Stood Still

Underneath the summer sky,
We both forgot to say goodbye,
With ice cream dripped upon our shirts,
Now sweetened sticky, oh how it hurts!

The clock just laughed, we lost track of time,
With silly jokes, and words that rhyme,
Every tick was made of fun,
In our world, we were the sun.

We danced around in grassy fields,
Stomped our feet as laughter yields,
The bubble of joy, it burst so loud,
Forgetting all, we felt so proud.

But as the sunset stole the day,
Time tiptoed in, it took you away,
Yet in my heart, you'll always stay,
In memories where time's at play.

Heartstrings Twined Like Vines

In a garden full of cheerful blooms,
Let's twirl 'round like silly looms,
Our hearts entwined, just like those strings,
Creating laughter, oh what joy it brings!

You told a joke, it made a mess,
Your giggle turned into a guess,
With petals flying in the breeze,
Nature laughed, and so did we.

Through tangled paths, we skipped and hopped,
With silly dreams that never flopped,
In every twist and every turn,
Our love ignited, brightly burned.

So here we stand, vines intertwined,
In this garden, laughter's defined,
With every moment, joy will climb,
Together, we dance, forever in rhyme.

Fables Told in Candlelight

Gather 'round, let tales embark,
With every flicker, we'll leave a mark,
In shadows cast, the humor grows,
As candlelight dances, creativity flows.

Once there was a girl, quite bold,
Who danced with grace, or so she'd told,
Tripping twice in her own parade,
Laughter echoed, she wasn't dismayed.

And then a lad, with grand ideas,
Tried to impress, but spilled his beers,
With every blunder, the night was bright,
Fables born in the gentle light.

So raise a glass to silly dreams,
In every tale, pure joy redeems,
With laughter echoing through the night,
Candlelit stories ignite our delight.

The Last Cup of Coffee Shared

In a cafe where spillages lay,
Two cups on a table, the sunlight's ballet.
Laughter slipped out like cream in a brew,
While crumbs told their tales of the sweet and the blue.

One sip turned a chuckle, then spilled on the floor,
As stories of exes began to uproar.
"Remember that time?" and they both cracked up,
While shouting the name of a long-gone pup.

Beneath the Cherry Blossom Hues

Petals like wishes drift down from above,
Two hearts in a tangle, mistaken for love.
"Is that your pink tie? Or my cherry-flavored pie?"
They giggled and snorted, both reaching to sigh.

A bird on the branch let out quite a squawk,
As they argued if it was time for a walk.
With blossoms a-falling, they practiced their dance,
Tripping in petals, a whimsical chance.

Whispered Promises in the Shadows

In a corner so cozy, secrets unwound,
Two friends in the dark, chuckles abound.
"Did you see that guy? He really was bold!"
"His dance moves are ancient, or so I've been told!"

Promises murmured in hushed tones of glee,
As they plotted their futures 'neath the old oak tree.
One dreams of adventure, the other of cheese,
In laughter, they wander, their worries at ease.

Gleaming Memories on the Horizon

On a shore where the waves met the brightening sky,
Two friends built a castle, their laughter ran high.
"Look! A dog in shades!" Let out a loud squeal,
As sand stuck to laughter revealed how they feel.

The tide rolled in quickly, as it often does,
Their masterpiece wobbled, a triumphant fuss.
With sunlight a-blinking and giggles in tow,
They knew it was perfect, despite the water's flow.

Petals on a Forgotten Path

A cat in a hat danced in delight,
Chasing butterflies, oh what a sight!
Tripped over petals, then tumbled down,
Wore a flower crown, like a silly clown.

A squirrel threw nuts, like confetti in air,
While the dog did a jig without any care.
Laughter erupted from all around,
As they rolled in the grass, not a worry found.

The wind carried giggles on soft fluffy gusts,
Chasing the shadows, fulfilling their trust.
With flowers in hair and mud on their feet,
They danced through the day, with joy bittersweet.

As evening approached, they ended their play,
Sang silly songs all the way to the bay.
With petals off track and laughter so bright,
The journey was silly, a pure pure delight.

Piecing Together Yesterday

A puzzle of mishaps, at first all was fine,
Until the dog snatched a slice of the pie.
I tripped on a shoe, slipped on the floor,
And spilled a whole jug, oh what a chore!

Mom laughed so hard, we cleaned up the mess,
While Dad found it funny, though slightly distressed.
Then came Grandma with a wink and a grin,
"Let's bake another! Come on, let's begin."

The eggs rolled away, as if seeking escape,
While flour turned rogue, adopting strange shape.
With giggles aplenty and batter in hair,
The kitchen was buzzing; we didn't care.

Yesterday's chaos was laughter-filled gold,
Each mishap a story, a memory to hold.
So we pieced together, each joyful today,
Mixing laughter and love in our own silly way.

Morning Dew and Sweet Reminders

The rooster crowed, but lost his cool,
He thought it was Monday; played the fool.
Chickens all clucked, in a feathery mess,
Running in circles, in a feathery dress.

The sun peeked over, with a yawn and a stretch,
While flowers unfurled, with colors attached.
A bee buzzed by, with plans quite absurd,
Decided to dance, not gather—how heard!

A butterfly landed on the dog's wiggly tail,
And off they both flew, down a silly trail.
The dew on the grass sparkled bright as can be,
While laughter rippled like waves in the sea.

Morning's mischief a canvas of cheer,
As memories bloomed, full of giggles, not fear.
With each sweet reminder, as light as a tune,
The laughter carried us, morning to noon.

A Canvas of Mixed Emotions

A painter set forth, with colors all bright,
To capture the chaos, the day and the night.
But splatters and drips made the canvas askew,
With laughter and smiles splashed in with the blue.

The cat chased a brush, that swished like a bug,
While the dog dipped a paw, thought it a hug.
Mixing up colors that made no true sense,
Twists of confusion—oh, what suspense!

Emotions ran wild, with each stroke a jest,
My art turned into a riotous quest.
Laughter erupted with each silly glide,
As faces turned pink from the paint and the pride.

By sunset's embrace, the masterpiece shone,
A riot of colors uniquely our own.
In mixed-up emotions, we all found our bliss,
A canvas of laughter, an artistic twist.

www.ingramcontent.com/pod-product-compliance
Lightning Source LLC
Chambersburg PA
CBHW051650160426
43209CB00004B/867